Ichiro Suzuki

Revised Edition

By Jeff Savage

Lerner Publications Company • Minneapolis

Lerner Publications Company
A division of Lerner Publishing Group, Inc.
241 First Avenue North
Minneapolis, MN 55401 USA

For reading levels and more information, look up this title at www.lernerbooks.com.

Library of Congress Cataloging-in-Publication Data

Savage, Jeff, 1961–
    Ichiro Suzuki / by Jeff Savage. – 2nd Rev. ed.
      pages   cm. — (Amazing athletes)
    Includes index.
    ISBN: 978–1–4677–2641–2 (pbk. : alk. paper)
    ISBN: 978–1–4677–2642–9 (eBook)
    1. Suzuki, Ichiro, 1973– —Juvenile literature. 2. Baseball players—Japan—Biography—
Juvenile literature. I. Title.
GV865.S895S38 2014
796.357092—dc23 [B]   2013022640

Manufactured in the United States of America
1 – BP – 12/31/13

TABLE OF CONTENTS

Fans hold up a sign to encourage Ichiro.

4,000!

Ichiro Suzuki stood in the **batter's box** on August 22, 2013. The New York Yankees **outfielder** raised his arm. He pointed his bat at the sky and adjusted his jersey. Cameras clicked all around Yankee Stadium. Ichiro could make history with one swing.

The **veteran** had begun his baseball career in Japan in 1993. He played in his home country until 2000. During that time, Ichiro racked up 1,278 hits. He kept on hitting when he joined **Major League Baseball (MLB)** in 2001. He collected 2,721 more hits with the Yankees and the Seattle Mariners. This gave him a total of 3,999 hits at the highest levels of baseball.

Ichiro getting his first MLB hit in 2001.

Ichiro lines a hit in the bottom of the first inning. It was his 4,000th hit.

Pete Rose collected the most hits in MLB history (4,256). Ty Cobb has the second most (4,189).

He needed just one more to reach 4,000.

Only two players had collected as many as 4,000 hits in a career. Ichiro wanted to be the third.

He swung at the next pitch. He slapped the ball to the left side of the infield. It streaked to the outfield for a **single**. Ichiro had done it!

Ichiro *(wearing number 31)* celebrating with his teammates after his big hit.

Ichiro takes off his helmet and bows to fans after his first-inning hit.

The fans roared as Ichiro's teammates came out of the **dugout**. The Yankees players gathered around him on first base. They smiled and hugged Ichiro. Everyone was happy for the outfielder.

Ichiro was happy to have reached 4,000 hits. But he was especially glad that his teammates were there to share the moment. "I wasn't expecting when my teammates came out to first base," he said. "That was very special."

Ichiro, like kids all over Japan, joined a local Little League team to improve his baseball skills.

LEARNING THE GAME

Ichiro Suzuki was born October 22, 1973, in Kasugai, Japan. His first name is pronounced "ee-chee-ro." It means "first boy." Some say it also translates to "fast man."

Baseball is a popular sport in Japan, just as it is in America. Ichiro grew up in Nagoya and began playing with a baseball at the age of three. He rode his bicycle to elementary school and earned good grades. By second grade, he had completely fallen in love with baseball. He wanted to become a great player someday.

Japan, Ichiro's home country, is long and narrow. Ichiro's hometown of Nagoya is a big port city in central Japan where cloth, bicycles, and other products are made.

Ichiro joined his hometown Little League team. His father, Nobuyuki, became coach of the team. The team played only on Sundays. Ichiro knew he would need to play more than once a week to become great. So he and his father practiced every day after school. Ichiro worked hard on fundamentals such as hitting and baserunning.

An American schoolteacher introduced baseball to Japan in the 1870s. By the 1930s, the first professional Japanese leagues were in place. By the 1970s, when Ichiro started to become interested in baseball, the sport was well established.

Ichiro went to Aiko-Dai Meiden High School in Nagoya. He was a star on the school's baseball team. Twice he played in Koshien, the national high school baseball tournament in Japan. He impressed Japanese professional

scouts. Upon his graduation from high school, he was **drafted** by a team called the Orix Blue Wave as their right fielder.

Ichiro pitched in Koshien, the Japanese national high school baseball tournament.

Kobe, home of the Orix Blue Wave, is a huge city in central Japan. Ichiro still lives there in the off-season.

TURNING PRO

Ichiro had achieved his dream. He had become a pro baseball player. The Blue Wave played their home games in Kobe, a port city of nearly two million people. But before Ichiro could join the Blue Wave, he played in the **minor leagues**. There he learned how to hit pro pitching and perfected his sprint around the bases.

In 1993, Ichiro was called up to the Blue Wave. He quickly became a star in Japan. In Ichiro's first full season, he set a record with 210 hits. He led the league in batting average and was named the 1994 Japanese Pacific League's Most Valuable Player (MVP).

Ichiro improved his blinding speed around the bases in the minor leagues.

The next year, he led in batting average again. He also ranked first in runs batted in (RBI) and **stolen bases**. He was named league MVP again. In 1996, he led the Blue Wave to the Japan Series championship. He was an easy choice as league MVP again.

With the Orix Blue Wave, Ichiro became an outstanding batter. He won the Japanese Pacific League's batting award seven times in a row.

Ichiro's style stood out in many ways. He threw from right field with his right hand, yet he batted left-handed.

In the batter's box, he aimed his bat toward the pitcher. He looked as if he was about to duel with a sword. He swung with quick wrists and a slashing swing.

Ichiro was equally skilled in the outfield of the Blue Wave team. Here, he slides to make a catch.

Ichiro followed up his hits with incredible running speed. He not only reached first base quickly but was often able to steal additional bases.

Upon making contact, Ichiro put on a burst of speed to reach first base. And in the outfield, Ichiro's ability to chase down balls was matched by his powerful throwing arm.

Ichiro had become the most popular baseball player in Japan. The team's souvenir shops sold Ichiro cups, key chains, baseballs, jerseys, T-shirts, posters, stickers, notebooks, pins, and flags. He was known throughout Japan simply as Ichiro. His coach even changed the name on the back of his uniform from Suzuki to Ichiro.

In a game against a team from Osaka, Japan, Ichiro made an incredible catch to save the game.

Ichiro thanked his many Japanese fans at his last game as a Blue Wave. He had decided to join the American major leagues.

AN INSTANT HIT

In 2000, Ichiro won the Japanese batting title for the seventh straight time. He had become so famous that a letter addressed simply to "Ichiro, Japan" would reach his mailbox. A poll named him the most recognizable person in Japan, just ahead of the emperor of Japan.

But Ichiro wanted to play baseball in North America, where baseball had begun. Many major-league baseball teams wanted him. The Seattle Mariners offered the most money. They paid $13 million to the Blue Wave and $15 million to Ichiro. Ichiro was sad to leave Japan but excited to come to America. "I go, but another star soon will replace me," Ichiro said.

Ichiro was all smiles after signing his contract to play for the Seattle Mariners in December of 2000.

Ichiro meets the press after a workout with the Mariners in Seattle in January 2001.

When Ichiro joined the Mariners for the 2001 season, seven Japanese pitchers were on major-league rosters. However, Ichiro became the first non-pitcher to join Major League Baseball. Some predicted that Ichiro would do well. Others thought he would be a bust. "Sometimes I am nervous, sometimes anxious," said Ichiro. "But I want to challenge a new world."

Ichiro was an instant hit. He had his first great game on Opening Day. A few days later, he hit a game-winning home run in extra innings. The next day, he made a laserlike throw from right field to nail a base runner at third base.

Seattle fans got used to seeing Ichiro's incredible catches and throws from right field.

Ichiro throws to first base during a 2001 Yankees versus Mariners game.

The Mariners won 116 games to tie the major league record for most victories in one season. Ichiro hit .350 to win the league batting title. He also led the league in hits and stolen bases.

Ichiro steals a base against the Texas Rangers.

In the playoffs, he batted .600 through five games to lead the Mariners past the Cleveland Indians. Seattle was one step from the World Series for the first time in history. But the team's magical season ended against the Yankees.

Ichiro runs fast to first base.

THE HITS KEEP COMING

Ichiro continued to rack up hits. In 2002, he finished fourth in the league in batting with a .321 average. In 2003, he had more than 200 hits for the third year in a row.

The 2004 season proved to be Ichiro's best yet. He set the all-time record for most hits in a year with 262. The previous record had stood since 1920!

In 2007, Ichiro was voted to the All-Star Game for the seventh year in a row. He hit singles in each of his first two **at bats**. Then he hit a ball high off the outfield wall. He ran around the bases for an **inside-the-park home run**. Ichiro was named MVP of the game. "I'm really happy," he said. "It was a fun All-Star Game."

Ichiro takes a powerful swing at the 2007 All-Star Game.

Ichiro had 214 hits in 2010. This was the 10th year in a row that he had at least 200 hits. No other player in MLB history had so many hits for so many years in a row.

Seattle's first two games of the 2012 season were held in Japan. They played against the Oakland Athletics. The Mariners won the first game, 3–1. Ichiro had four hits. "It was very special to open in Japan," he said.

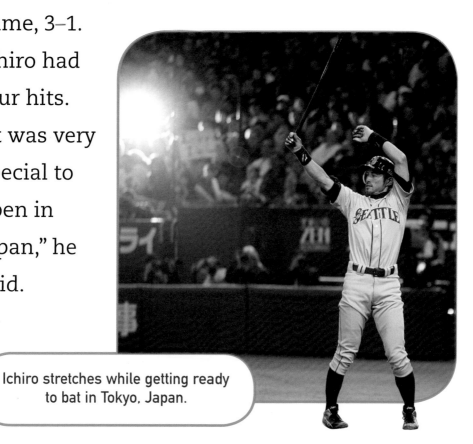

Ichiro stretches while getting ready to bat in Tokyo, Japan.

Seattle fans were sad to see Ichiro leave the Mariners.

The Mariners were not a good team in 2012. Near the end of July, they traded Ichiro to the Yankees. He was happy to join a winning team. But he was upset about leaving Seattle after more than 11 seasons. "When I imagined taking off the Mariner uniform, I was overcome with sadness," he said.

Ichiro misses Seattle. But he has continued to shine in New York. He is a baseball legend in two countries.

Selected Career Highlights

2013 Reached 4,000 hits for his career

2012 Traded to the New York Yankees

2011 Collected 184 hits to end streak of 200-hit seasons

2010 Collected 200 or more hits for 10th straight season

2009 Collected 200 or more hits for ninth straight season

2008 Collected 200 or more hits for eighth straight season

2007 Collected 200 or more hits for seventh straight season

2006 Won his sixth Gold Glove award

2005 Won his fifth Gold Glove award

2004 Set all-time record (262) for hits in a season

2003 Finished second in hits in American League

2002 Won his second Gold Glove award

2001 Won American League batting title
Won his first Gold Glove award
Named American League's Most Valuable Player
Named American League's Rookie of the Year

Glossary

at bats: players' turns at batting

batter's box: the rectangular area on either side of home plate in which the batter stands while at bat

drafted: to be chosen from a selected group to play on a professional sports team

dugout: the enclosed area with a long bench along either side of a baseball field. Players and coaches sit or stand in the dugout during a game.

inside-the-park home run: a hit that does not go over the outfield fence but still allows a batter to run all the way around the bases to score a run

Major League Baseball (MLB): the top level of baseball in the United States

minor leagues: the lower leagues where young players improve their playing skills. It is one step below the major leagues.

outfielder: a person who plays in the outfield

scouts: people who review the playing skills of young players

single: a hit that allows a batter to safely reach first base

stolen bases: when runners advance to the next base while the pitcher throws the ball to home plate

veteran: a player with more than one year of experience

Further Reading & Websites

Kennedy, Mike, and Mark Stewart. *Long Ball: The Legend and Lore of the Home Run*. Minneapolis: Millbrook Press, 2006.

Leigh, David S. *Ichiro Suzuki*. Minneapolis: Twenty-First Century Books, 2004.

Official MLB Site
http://www.mlb.com/home
Visit the official Major League Baseball website to find game details, biographies of players, and information about baseball.

The Official Site of the New York Yankees
http://newyork.yankees.mlb.com/index.jsp?c_id=nyy
The New York Yankees official site includes the team schedule and game results. Visitors can also find late-breaking news, biographies of Ichiro Suzuki and other players and coaches, and much more.

Sports Illustrated Kids
http://www.sikids.com
The *Sports Illustrated Kids* website covers all sports, including baseball.

Index

Photo Acknowledgments

The images in this book are used with the permission of: © Rich Schultz /Getty Images, p. 4; © Otto Greule Jr/Hulton Archive/Getty Images, p. 5; © Mike Stobe/Getty Images, p. 6; © Ron Antonelli/Getty Images, pp. 7, 8; © Robert Holmes/CORBIS, p. 10; © Steve Kaufman/CORBIS, p. 11; © Kyodo News Agency, pp. 13, 16, 17, 18, 19, 20, 21; © Michael S. Yamashita/CORBIS, p. 14; © Dan Levine/AFP/Getty Images, p. 22; © Otto Greule Jr/Getty Images, p. 23; Jim Bryant UPI Photo Service/Newscom, p. 24; AP Photo/Elaine Thompson, pp. 25, 29; © Koji Watanabe/Getty Images, pp. 26, 28; © Jeff Gross/Getty Images, p. 27; © Reuters/CORBIS, p. 30.

Front Cover: © Jim McIsaac/Getty Images.

Main body text set in Caecilia LT Std 55 Roman 16/28.
Typeface provided by Adobe Systems.